Have You Counted the Stars?

Memoir of a Holocaust Orphan's Survival and Success

Simon Steil

Washington, DC

Via Publishing

9039 Sligo Creek Pkwy, Suite 1114 Silver Spring, Maryland 20901

Copyright © Simon Steil, heirs, 2020

Published by Via Publishing, 2020

All rights reserved. No part of this publication may be reproduced, distributed, or transmitted in any form or by any means, including photocopying, recording, or other electonic or mechanical methods, without the prior written permission of the publisher, except in the case of brief quotations embodied in critical reviews and certain other non commercial uses permited by copyright law.

Printed in the United States of America

10 9 8 7 6 5 4 3 2 1

LIBRARY OF CONGRESS CATALOGING-IN-PUBLICATION DATA

Steil, Simon

Have You Counted the Stars? Memoir of a Holocaust Orphan's Survival and Success/ Simon Steil
p. cm.

ISBN: 978-0-9960722-8-1

Written by Simon Steil

Edited by Rachel Miranda Feingold

Cover Design by Laura Kane

ACKNOWLEDGEMENTS

Douglas Steil – The youngest of my loving sons, and the project manager of this memoir, who helped to compile details and ensured we kept moving forward

Sylvain Brachfeld – Author of several books on Belgium's hidden children during World War II that helped me with my research. These volumes in particular helped to explain many memories that I carried over the years without knowing their meanings:

> *Ils n'ont pas eu ces gosses: L'histoire de plus de 500 enfants juifs sans parents fichés à la Gestapo et placés pendant l'occupation allemande dans les homes de l'association des juifs de Belgique (You Didn't Get These Children: The history of the more than 500 orphaned Jewish children taken by the Gestapo and placed during the German occupation in the homes of the Jewish Association of Belgium).*

> *Merci de Nous Avoir Sauvés. Temoignages d'Enfants Juifs Caches en Belgique (Thank you for Saving Us. Testimonies of Jewish Children Hidden in Belgium)*

> *The Brachfeld Family Book, A Gift of Life: The Deportation and the Rescue of the Jews in Occupied Belgium (1940-1944)*

Serge Klarsfeld and Maxime Steinberg, *Memorial de la déportation des juifs de Belgique (Memorial of the Deportation of the Jews of Belgium)*. I found the names of all deported Jews and a history of the deportation trains in this book.

Alexander Dunai – the initial researcher on the ground in Lviv, Ukraine who helped to search the local archives for details of the Steil family

Errol Schneegurt – A cousin who helped coordinate and compile the family genealogy research

Yad Vashem – this is Israel's Holocaust Museum and archive, an important resource for my research

United States Holocaust Memorial Museum – Their archives, too, provided important contributions to my research, and as a registered survivor, I was invited to attend the opening ceremonies, an emotional and memorable event for me.

Joan Steil – Wife, mother, friend, and partner of fifty years

Marck Steil – My dear brother, who I hardly knew and barely remember

Adolph and Eliza Steil – My loving parents, members of a once large, very successful, and brilliant family

Berta and Jules Henrard – The couple who hid me during the war in Perwez, Belgium at great risk to themselves. They loved me like a son and were kind enough to give me up to the Red Cross authorities after the war in 1948.

Aunt Eugenia – My mother's sister, who had only arrived to Belgium a year before being sent to Auschwitz

Emile and Adele Finel – My generous aunt and uncle who visited me at the orphanage every weekend after the war, and eventually alerted other relatives of my whereabouts, Mollie and Hyman Esig, who lived in the US

Mollie and Hyman Esig – My aunt and uncle who sponsored me to come to the US and housed and supported me from 1950 – 1959

A.B. Cornelius – Led the AJB (Association of Jews in Belgium) orphanage where I lived after being taken from my home in Antwerp, Belgium

Robert and Susan Spear – My good friend from the YMHA in Manhattan and his wife, who loved and supported me while I was a young adult in the US

Rachel Miranda Feingold – Developmental editor of this memoir

FOREWORD

The research for this book unfolded through a combination of good fortune and my own persistence in piecing together the picture of my life and that of my family. After being orphaned during World War II, I was reclaimed in 1950 by a relative living in the United States. I was twelve years old at the time. Certain formalities were required in obtaining my travel documentation, including a US passport and visa, and the Belgian government separation papers. When I traveled from the orphanage to a Belgian passport office to obtain the necessary information, I spotted a file folder containing documents and photographs of my family members, for whom I had no personal information nor images since being separated from them eight years earlier. It was in this way that I learned what my parents looked like, along with my date of birth and the proper way to spell my last name, which had been listed as "Stein" before that. My travel papers were prepared for me then, but I was never offered the contents of the folder. Still, the idea of recovering it was always on my mind.

Over the years, I continued to request from the Belgian authorities the material in the passport folder I had seen. After the internet got up and running, Jewishgen.com came online in 1990 with specific Jewish information indexed from national and international sources, and I began to assemble genealogical documents for my mother, my father, and my aunt's sister, including birth, marriage, and death certificates. Internet searches highlighted numerous Belgian Jewish organizations involved in survivor information. When I finally contacted the recommended organizations, I obtained a voluminous amount of material, including the mandatory updates required from citizens such as changes in residence and information from the original German occupation listing all my family members and all Jewish residents of the city of Antwerp.

The Germans, ever efficient, used the citizens' information to assign numbers to those they planned to deport in the future, and expected them to voluntarily show up for transportation to the then-unknown death camps. Prior to boarding the railcars, people were stripped of their personal belongings: this of course included my father, whose only remaining proof of his existence was a permit for permanent residency in Belgium that the Germans confiscated. It wasn't until 1980 that I found out my father had been conscripted to a TODT work camp in Normandy, and my mother had spent time as a victim-patient of Dr. Mengele before she died. These new revelations prompted my first return to Europe since coming to America thirty years before. Details about my visit are in the body of this book.

The US Holocaust Memorial Museum opened its doors in 1993, and I was invited to attend the survivors' preview. The building resembled a factory that evoked the death camps in its design. Through that event, I made a friend named Flo Singer, a greeter at the preview who had come from the Ukraine, suggesting that our families' fates had followed a similar trajectory.

In the early 1990s, I also recovered my father's permanent residency certification, the last document he ever signed. In 1995, I found the book *Ils N'ont Pas Eu Ces Gosses* (*They Did Not Get These Children*) which added more detail to my memories and my history. I realized why one of my orphanages had been called "La Bas" (meaning "over there"): it was because they did not want the name to point toward its location.

FOREWORD

I also understood that the reason Jewish orphan children were protected in Belgium was because the Belgian queen mother was from the German royal house (Saxe-Coburg-Gotha). She used her connections with the German military to get certain dispensations for Belgian-born Jewish orphans of adults who had been sent to the camps, securing the right for Belgian Jews to set up and run orphanages to protect the children until they were fourteen years old. Another memory of mine suddenly made sense, in which I repeatedly had flashlights shone in my face at night while asleep: the SS was searching for children over foutreen to deport to the camps, and because they kept such careful records, they knew exactly where each child was being kept.

I wanted badly to obtain data from the city of Lvov—where my parents came from—and I was first able to accomplish this in 1999 when I connected to a resident of the city named Alexander Dunai who was willing to do to a search of the Ukrainian archives for a fee. The key word to search was the family name of Steil. After a short period of anticipation, I received a three-page letter containing a list of the members of the many Steil families who had lived in Lvov. The three translated letters from the Ukraine, and the numbers of Steil family members listed there, increased my curiosity about their fate in the *Judenrein* of World War II.

II.

Following the start of the deportations, the previous assignment by the Germans of deportation numbers and train assignments to each person—without consideration of keeping families together—resulted in children being left alone. Intervention by the Belgian Queen with the German military authorities had resulted in permission to establish several Jewish orphanages that were run by Belgian Jewish natives and funded by native Jewish organizations:

1. Orphelinats Israelite of Antwerp [Anvers] et Bruxelles
2. Home de Wezenbeek-Ophem
3. Home d'Aische-en-Refaile also known as La-Bas
4. Home de Linkebeek
5. Two homes called "Moineaux" at Uccle and Etterbeek

Presumably, the Germans allowed these children to remain because they knew that any time the orphanages could be liquidated and the children transported to the death camp of Auschwitz.

As the war was ending, the liquidation of Jews became the highest priority of the Nazis, resulting in the deportation of the children from one of the homes. The home at La-Bas was also scheduled to be emptied but the Belgian underground were forewarned, and the result was that the children were hidden among the population of the surrounding villages. I was told the story by some of the people whom I visited in October 1980 with my wife, Joan.

As soon as the children were taken to the villages, the first ones selected were the oldest, since the farmers were in need of help because many of their own sons were still war prisoners in Germany. As for the smallest and youngest, they were allocated by the mayor to the people of the town. I was taken in by Berta and Jules Henrard who hid me and kept me in the town of Perwez until 1948 when we children were gathered by HIAS (the Hebrew Immigrant Aid Society) after the war and I was placed with Mr. Tiefenbruner in two orphanages, first in Brussels and when that closed, in Antwerp.

In Perwez during the war, I was required to remain inside the grocery store run by the Henrards, and received a dressing-down if I so much as raised the curtains to see outside. I remember one incident in which I was peering outside when a Gestapo truck pulled up at a house I thought was at some distance away. Many years later when I revisited Perwez, I recognized this distance was much closer than I remembered, and I understood their worry at the time.

Now to return to the genealogy search: It is interesting to note that on Jewishgen.com, all records had the same format in terms of the headings required and the name of the parents; the names of the grandparents were also included at times. This allowed family trees to be established and family connections made. The records also commented whether the births were legal or the child was "illegitimate," a frequent occurrence due to the fact that any marriage had to be performed by civil authorities for the offspring to be considered legal. A religious marriage and the subsequent births were recorded as illegitimate, with a note indicating the status of the child and the mother; the father could also volunteer his name. These detailed records were duplicated in all the towns and cities so that one copy could be sent to the capital city archives of the country, and were later preserved on the internet.

When I was getting ready to immigrate to the United States at the age of twelve, the authorities required that I obtain documentation at a Belgian government office which, I noted at the time, had significant photographic and written documentation of my family that I had never seen before. So at the beginning of my efforts, I was focused on obtaining that file. The Belgian file cleared up what my name actually was, since before that I had been called both Steil and Stein. Now that I also knew the birth place of my parents, I could fund a search of the Ukrainian records which focused on those people with the same last name. From the same file, I also obtained the names of my parents, brother, and aunt. My family at the beginning of World War II resided at the Antwerp address of Lange Kievitstraat 46, a Jewish neighborhood, and consisted of my father, Adolf; my mother, Eliza; my brother, Marck; and later, my aunt, Eugenia. There were nine years' difference between my brother and me, and this was explained by my father's plan to leave Lvov and establish himself in Belgium first, and then bring the family back together—though I only understood this later.

Further explanation of my father's search for a better family life is written in the history of the Jewish people's battle against anti-Semitism in Eastern Europe. The change in living conditions in Lvov under the new Polish government was significantly harsher than before World War I, when Emperor Franz Joseph ruled with a very mild and benign hand, allowing the empire, made up of many civilizations and races with their own beliefs, to be semi-independent. This situation changed under Polish rule—for example, all written and spoken communication had to be in Polish, whereas previously in Lvov the German language had been used in daily and official speech, schools, and correspondence.

So it seems that my father, like so many, many others, left the area and decided to start a new life in Belgium. In Europe, people's locations are very well documented as is any change in residence. My father's time in Belgium and his activities during the ten or so years he

FOREWORD

spent alone can be traced by these documents, as well as the labors he undertook to support himself and finally obtain permission to reside in Belgium. I arrived on the scene two years before the invasion of the low countries.

The dates and numbers assigned to my family members for their deportations to Auschwitz, which the German authorities gave to the deportation/passenger trains, were important because they allowed me to assign dates to some of the memories that I carried with me for many years but could not place specifically within a timeline before.

My aunt Eugenia Steil, sister to my father, was the first to be deported. She was born in Lvov on January 31, 1902 and had just arrived in Belgium in the late nineteen thirties. The German authorities

My aunt, Eugenia Steil

were very efficient in assigning dates for the deportations very early after their conquest of the low countries, a capability made possible because of their use of captured American data equipment. The assigned convoy/passenger number for my aunt was III/207.

My brother, Marck, born in Lvov on September 5, 1929, was assigned the deportation convoy/passenger number of XIV/641. My mother, Eliza Meiseles Steil, born in Lvov on March 31, 1902, was assigned the convoy/passenger number of XX/1527.

My mother, Eliza Steil, with Marck

My brother, Marck Steil

FOREWORD

The convoy departed Belgium on September 20, 1943 and arrived at Auschwitz on September 22, 1943. This date sets a marker of my being separated from my mother and from our residence at the address of 46 Lange Kievitstraats in Antwerp. My father, Adolf Steil, born in Lvov on October 28, 1898, was assigned the convoy/passenger number of XXII/20. This convoy was unique for it consisted of two parts: conscripted workers from Antwerp and Liege evacuated from the Dannes-Camiers labor camps in France, and raffle prisoners being held in Breendronk, Malines, Belgium. The large-scale deportations started in 1942, but my father had already been impacted, as he may have volunteered earlier on. In order to begin the construction of the Atlantic Wall, the Germans had requisitioned laborers from the conquered countries, since their own workers were in short supply in Germany, as the eligible manpower was serving in the military. In order to avoid the looming threat of relocation to the east, Jews from Belgium volunteered to go to France and work for German companies with pay. The Germans led and directed the work with the TODT organization, which was responsible for the design and construction of many concrete-reinforced structures, as well as all other trades.

My father, Adolf Steil

Many German companies participated with labor furnished by TODT. Labor camps to shelter the workers were located all along the coastal defenses, as needed.

Belgian legal residency pass giving my father permission to remain. The document was clearly not honored by officials and it was the last item seized from Adolf Steil before he was deported.

From the German transportation documentation, I was able to establish that my father was assigned to the Dannes-Camiers Jewish camp. During one of my visits to the town, in the "Hotel de Ville" as it is locally called, I found out that a resident had written two large volumes describing the history of the camps, and the relations of the townspeople with the victims of both Jewish and non-Jewish camps. The volumes included plans and daily activities. The Jewish laborers were required to work for seven days a week, while the non-Jewish laborers only worked five days a week. Further, only the Jews were restricted at all times to their camp while the other members were free to rest and obtain food. Hunger was a constant, for the townspeople could not give any form of nourishment to the Jews in the camp. The work days were long—at times through the day and night when concrete was to be poured—and the concrete structure had to be totally completed in one period of time; it could not be stopped in the middle.

The ultimate fate of the Jewish conscripted workers was decided by the racial laws and the Nazis' mission to destroy the Jewish race. The Atlantic wall was far from complete, labor was in short supply for the TODT organization, yet the destruction of the Jewish race took precedence above any and all construction efforts. It is well known that the supply trains and passenger troop transport trains required by the German military were taken over for the transport of the Jews to the death camps, such as Auschwitz, Belzec, and many others. The workers of the Jewish camp of Dannes-Camiers were deported on the XXII transport, September 20, 1943.

When I lived with my aunt and uncle in the United States, I was only vaguely aware that we had other relatives in New York. It was not until I obtained data from the internet that I realized my aunt had a sister named Rosalie, one of the many siblings of my grandmother, Hanna Finel. I identified the Schneegurt line of the family; my cousin Errol also pursued genealogy research, and some of his data has been included here.

We compared data and I learned that his grandmother and my aunt Mollie were sisters. He had much information, including a photograph of the matriarch Henne or Hanna Finel and her family in Lvov, that includes Errol's father and my aunt's children, Henry and Felicia. Errol also generated a Finel family tree, on which I have based the one below.

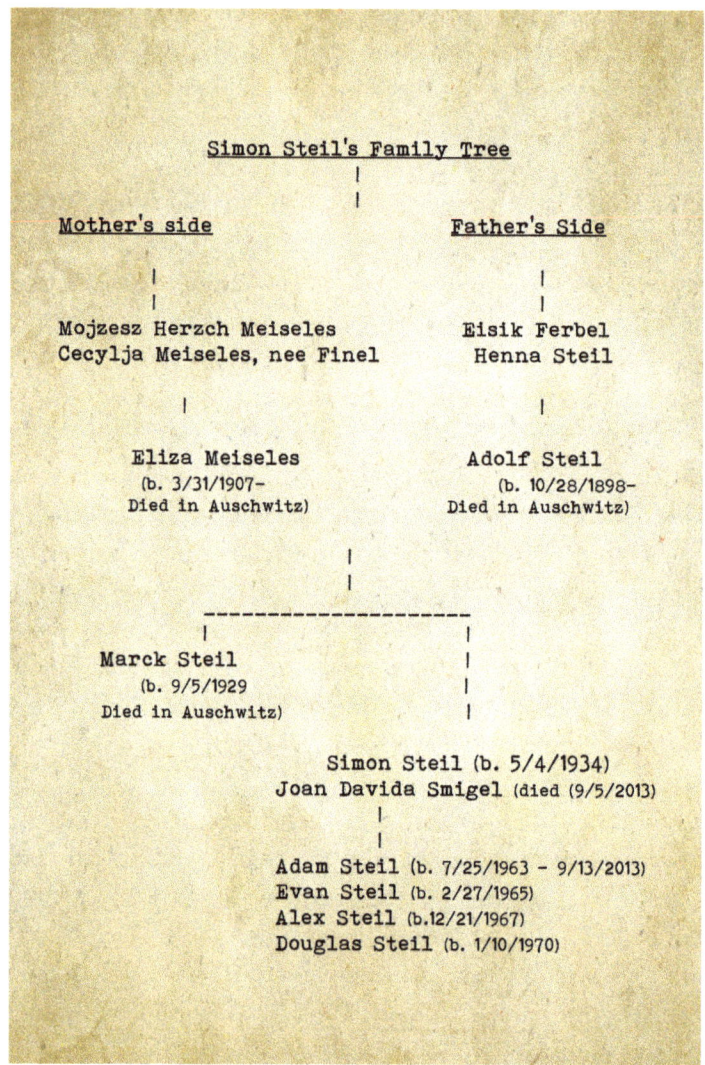

My family tree, begining with my grandparents

FOREWORD

In 1997, I was approached by Steven Spielberg's Shoah project to preserve the stories of Holocaust survivors, and was interviewed and videotaped, one among 70,000. Recounting the story was a very powerful and emotional process for me. In 1999, Yad Vashem came online, another exciting event because I could digitally search for information about my family and my background.

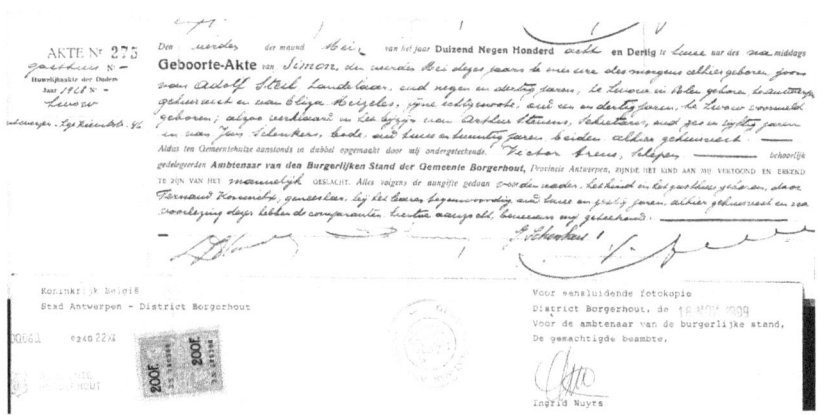

My birth certificate, recieved from the Belgian government in 1999

The genealogical revelations continue to this day: I just recently received the address of the first place I went after my parents were deported, what I came to think of as the "blue room," in Malines. I have kept at it, slowly assembling the picture of my family that I never had a chance to learn the usual way. Now I am writing it all down, so that future generations can know what it has taken me a lifetime to find out.

FOREWORD

PROLOGUE: LVOV

Lvov, Lwow, Lviv, and Lemberg. Why so many names for one city? The answer reveals the political struggles of the region and, ultimately, the reason for my father's immigration to Belgium.

The city's name changed every time it came under the rule of a different empire, kingdom, or republic with its own language and culture—an event that occurred frequently, due to Lvov's central location in the middle of many historical empires, each wanting control of the city and its surrounding lands. After the First Polish Partition in 1772, the city became part of the Habsburg Empire with the two divided parts of Poland at odds over the possession of the city and the region. Lemberg, as it was called under the Austrian-Hungarian empire, grew significantly through the influx of Germans and Austrians speaking Czech and resulting in the city developing an Austrian physical appearance, and becoming the third most populous city of the Polish Republic after World War I.

At the conclusion of World War I and with the Treaty of Versailles, the victorious Allies reconstituted Poland by incorporating the Galicia area along with the city as part of the Polish state. And so the Austrian-Hungarian (German) name of the city was changed to the Polish Lwow. At the same time, the Ukrainian Republic was declared on November 1, 1918. The result was the Polish-Ukrainian war.

Under Habsburg rule, Lvov was the cultural center for many

different nationalities: Polish, Ukrainian, and Jewish. After the establishment of Polish rule in 1919, the multicultural life in the city changed with strict policies such as the closing of Ukrainian-speaking schools, and the closing down of Ukrainian departments at Lvov University. The inhabitants of the western part of the city were mainly Polish, while the eastern part of the city and most of the rural region were Ukrainians. The Austrian Lvov census of 1910 noted that Jews constituted twenty-eight percent of the city population. The Jews of the city declared their neutrality in the fight for independence between the Polish and the Ukrainians, leading to chaos and pogroms on both sides, who equally viewed this stance of neutrality as being favorable to the others. The non-democratic rule of the Polish government impacted both Ukrainian and Jewish institutions which resulted, for example, in the limiting of public displays of Jewish and Ukrainian culture. Polish rule became very oppressive, including the mandatory use of the Polish language in government and educational institutions and the restriction of Yiddish use. There were many pogroms between the years of 1917 and 1921, and the living conditions of the Jews deteriorated.

I can only assume this situation was behind my father's decision to immigrate to Belgium. The records indicate that he arrived on October 18, 1929, and was living at 3 Consciencestraat, Antwerp by May 31, 1930. From October 18, 1929 to December 8, 1930 his address was 32 Diepenbeekstraat, Antwerp and from December 8, 1930 to April 4, 1931 at 33 V. der Meydenstraat, Antwerp. I don't know why he moved around so much. According to the official Belgian records, on August 22, 1930 he applied to the Belgian Minister in Warsaw for a three-month visa for my mother and my brother, Marck, then one year old.

From my mother's and brother's passport application forms, the genealogy line of the family was detailed as follows:

FOREWORD

My mother's father: Mojzesz Herzch Meiseles
My mother's mother: Cecylja Meiseles, née Finel
My father's father: Eisik Ferbel
My father's mother: Henna Steil

The information above was furnished to explain why my father has as his family name my grandmother's name of Steil instead of my grandfather's family name of Ferbel. His explanation was that at the time, the government required one to be married in a civil ceremony for the child to be given the father's name. In other words, a *religious* marriage ceremony would result in the official birth records denoting the child as a bastard. This could be rectified on the records by having the father acknowledge his responsibility. My mother's reason for the travel was to rejoin her husband. On December 19, 1930, my father requested a visa from the governor of the province of Anvers for unlimited residence in Belgium for my mother and brother.

The government required that it be notified of every change of address during one's lifetime by all residents, which is how I know that by May 4, 1938, our family address was 46 Lange Lievitstraat, Antwerp. It's also how I know that my aunt Eugenia had lived in Lemberg at Platz Theadora no. 2, but had moved to Krakow, Poland and resided at Stradom no. 17 until her departure for Belgium. She arrived in Belgium just thirteen days after the German invasion of Poland, on September 22, 1939.

SIMON STEIL

The Finel Family in Lvov, 1920s

1. DEPORTATIONS

I was born on May 4, 1938 in Borgenhout, Antwerp, Belgium. Because I was orphaned at an early age after my family was deported by the Nazis, I did not have the opportunity of living my history or knowing about my family. As an adult, I was determined to fill in the blanks of my life and give my children some clarity.

My childhood home: Lange Kievitstraat 46, Antwerp, Belgium

My first memory relating to the deportations was a Sabbath evening meal when German authorities interrupted our family gathering. The main room in our house had a large rear window overlooking the garden and I saw my older brother, Marck, who was in the garden at the time, caught by the Germans. At the same time, I heard heavy footsteps tramping on the roof; in my memory, it is a neighbor who allowed the roof incursion. The most memorable event was being hidden with an adult in a dark closet under the stairs. I cannot fully explain the dates or people involved, for I was only four years old at the time. According to the Belgian Service *Archives et Documentation* dated March 17, 2002, after that I was initially hidden in the home of a certain A.B. Cornelis, address of 27 Wolmaakt in Malines, until June 1943. I don't know how I got there, and I don't remember him. The only information I have is from an official letter from the Belgian Service, stating that I was there until June 1943.

Eliza Meiseles Steil, my mother

The only clear memory I have from this time is waking up in a blue-painted room full of cribs with many very young children in them. I believe this room was in a place run by Catholic nuns, also in Malines. It's also possible that we were at the home of Mr. Cornelis, the director of the orphanage. The nuns were at times very comforting and at times very severe. I remember having a large, infected swelling in the palm of my hand, which was gently taken care of by a nun.

Another incident I recall: we children were witnesses to an air battle between German and British airplanes, which ended with the British plane being shot down. For some reason, despite our youth, we were taken to see the crash site. I remember well the scene of total destruction: all that was left of the plane and the pilot was a large hole, filled with metal parts and many paper maps covered in blood. No attempt was ever made to recover the pilot; we were told he was to be covered over and the site noted.

The yard at the rear of the building had a field behind it in which grew large yellow sunflowers that were in full bloom at the time. Whenever I see the yellow of those flowers, it reminds me of that part of my life.

2. INTERIM HOMES

After my departure from A.B. Cornelis and the nuns, I was housed in Fort Breendonk, a fortress in Malines that had been taken over by German police to gather people for triage before their deportations. I believe that this move resulted from police harassment of the people from the Cornelis home. There were a lot of adults at Breendonk, and the floor was covered with straw that we slept on. The one important memory from my time there was that there was a piano, and people sang. I always remembered the first lines of one particular song:

A tu conte les etoiles dans le ciel radieux?
Have you counted the stars in the radiant sky?

Aische-en-Rafail Castle in 1943

Then came the time of my entrance to the orphanage at Aische-en-Refail, which stands clearly in my mind. It was a large country estate that had been allowed to fall into disrepair and needed significant fixing to be fit to shelter Jewish children whose parents had been deported. It was also called La-Bas, which means "over there"; this second name was given to the children to use when asked from where they came.

Significant repairs were started in January with the help of town laborers as well as some of the older children. The facility was under the patronage of the Belgian Queen Elizabeth, as were a number of others around the country.

An explanation is needed to understand the unique conditions that existed in the occupied lands. It is safe to say that these conditions varied depending on whether the lands were in Eastern or Western Europe. In the West, some populations were considered Aryan which ameliorated the occupation, whereas in the East the people were considered less than human. As for the Jewish population in Belgium, the fact that the royal family and the king had not fled to England, and the married queen had been from the German royal house of Saxe-Coburg-Gotha, resulted in the German military's willingness to defer to certain demands of the queen when it came to the issue of Belgian Jewish citizens and those who were not Belgian citizens but, like my family, had migrated to Belgium between the wars.

The Jewish population of Belgium was almost evenly divided between citizens and non-citizens, and the Belgian queen negotiated that initial deportations would consist of only non-Belgian citizens. Once the deportations started using assigned numbers, the groups were not always composed of complete families, and sometimes children were left by themselves. But again, with the aid of the queen, the Germans allowed the establishment and staffing of orphanages by the Jewish organizations of Belgium, a concession that might be taken as a humanitarian act, but could also be viewed as a way to easily gather and deport the children at a later time.

It is interesting to note that not all German organizations were aware of all the agreements made by the military authorities. In June of 1943, the Belgian underground learned that the Gestapo from Charleroi were going to raid the orphanages and deport all the children. The Jewish committees, which during the occupation had hidden many people in private houses and religious places such as convents and churches, recognized the danger and immediately dispersed the children. La Bas was near the village of Perwez, in the French-speaking part of Belgium, and that is where I was sent.

On my first return trip to Perwez, my wife, Joan, and I were invited to stay overnight in the house to the one I had lived in. The neighbors' house had in the past been a police station. Many long conversations over local wine allowed us to fill out some of the facts of how I came to be hidden in Perwez and by whom—one of only eleven Jewish children hidden in the village after the orphanage at Aische-en-Refail was dispersed. There had been local raids, called "raffles" by the Gestapo, and once the Jewish underground got word that one such raid was planned for the orphanage, the children were dispersed throughout the area before they could be deported. Eleven children from Aische-en-Refail were brought into the village and the mayor took charge. Voluntary requests by the townspeople to harbor the children resulted in the almost immediate selection of the oldest children.

Why the oldest children? The reason had to do with the war and the surrender of the Belgian king and government. The young men were absent because they were prisoners of war in Germany, and the farmers of the area were short of manpower and in desperate need of labor. The elder children could help on the farms and replace temporarily those who were missing.

As for the younger children, like me—I was five years old—I later learned that the mayor simply selected which townspeople would hide us. It is remarkable that the Henrards and so many others of the village jeopardized their lives by acting contrary to German laws.

School house in Perwez

Henrards' house in Perwez where I was hidden

My life with Jules and Berta Henrard until the liberation of the village of Perwez on September 9, 1945 was very fortunate: I never lacked for nourishment nor even unusual foods, because our next-door neighbors were butchers and had a slaughterhouse. Interestingly, the Germans allowed the people to have shotguns which they used in hunting for wild game. Many times, the next-door family passed extra game dishes that they did not need over the wall separating our two houses.

I was required to stay in the house during the days and nights, and was not even allowed to look outside by pushing the curtains aside. I remember once I sneaked a look outside and was severely reprimanded. At the time, a small pickup truck had pulled up in the village square and I noticed somebody being thrown into the back of the truck. Now I understand what they had been afraid of: the arrest of those hiding the Jews, and their deaths at the hands of the Germans.

During the hiding days, I helped in some mundane tasks such as bringing wood into the house from the fenced-in yard to provide heat for the house and for my bath, which I took in a large washtub. During a time of greater freedom, gardening was a positive activity to bring in fresh vegetables and fruits to supplement the daily allowances under the occupation. I should also not forget the pet rabbits that I nursed and took good care of.

My freedom initially lasted only for a period of about four months, because Perwez was located very close to the town of Bastogne, where the last great German offensive unfolded, giving the townspeople the feeling that the German army would return and wreak havoc. So, we all went back into hiding for the next three or four months until the allies had definitely won the battle and secured the retreat of the German army.

Thirty years after my immigration to the Unites States, I wanted very much to return and clear up some memories. These memories, though deep in my unconscious, were not tied to any facts but to incidents that I thought I remembered from a very young age. For example, I had seen that file in 1950 when I got my passport, and it included photographs of my family that I did not have. I wanted to find those pictures, but in those days, the internet did not even exist, and so any information I received came through the postal service, and often took years to uncover.

It took me thirty years to return because I did not have the funds before that: I married, had children, bought a house, built my career. But the mysteries had accumulated for all that time, and I wanted to find answers.

I was most eager to get back to Perwez, the town where I lived with Jules and Berta Henrard, the dearest people who had hidden me during the war.

Berta Henrard with me on her lap, next to Jules and daughters

I had remained in contact with them for a number of years, but the passing of time ultimately led to fewer letters, followed by a letter announcing their deaths. They had died within a short time of one another, and their son—a pharmacist in Perwez—contacted me to tell me the news. I had always hoped that we would meet again. The son, Louis, was the spitting image of his father, of whom I had kept a picture for all those years.

When I went back and saw his family, as well as the neighbors and many other people who remembered me, they welcomed me as if I had never left.

I planned my return with Joan and laid out a circular trip to cover as many cities as we could. I had spent twelve years in Belgium, and I wanted to explore the country of my birth. We planned to visit Bruges, Louvain, Brussels, Waterloo, and of course my home city of Antwerp.

We landed on a Friday, hours before Shabbat, so we went straight to a Jewish organization in Antwerp and I decided to inquire whether anyone knew of a family named Finel. Immediately, someone contacted relatives of the Finels, called Apfelbaum, and handed me the phone. I spoke with Henie Apfelbaum, who it turned out was a distant cousin of mine. Joan and I were invited to their vacation home on the North Sea in Blankenberge for the next day, which we would visit on our way to Perwez.

We needed to stop for the night, and we drove the rental car as far as the town of Wavre. Joan was an easy travel companion, for she was not one who needed an American-style hotel and was not excessively concerned with comfort and service, so we enjoyed many small local hotels and restaurants and heard lots of stories from the locals. The place in Wavre was run by a mother and son, who ran the hotel and bar/restaurant respectively; after this trip, we always made it our first stop in Belgium. The one thing we could never forget was the rich delicious hot chocolate with our breakfasts.

When we arrived at the house the next day, we were greeted warmly and saw that there were many other people there for the traditional Shabbat coffee and cake. The people gathered there were well-dressed and clearly affluent. Henie was in the diamond business, and I realized how successful he was when I was introduced to the governor of the province of Antwerp. We sat down to talk about our families and our family history.

I felt great anticipation at the thought of entering the Grand Place of Perwez, the central square that is a common feature of most cities in Europe, whether large or small. Before the war, Perwez was a town where many important highways came together, and this resulted in savage bombings at the start of the war. After the liberation, I was able to freely roam the town and play in the bombed-out structures with other children.

I cannot describe the feeling that I had at seeing the difference between these images that were embedded deep in my memory, and the reality of the many rebuilt streets in a fashion that must have mimicked the original structures. Many sites of my time in Perwez until 1948 were still there to visit: I remembered the quarry where I swam many times, the movie house where I saw my first movies—the original Jean Cocteau versions of *The Beauty and the Beast* and *Snow White*. Modernity also changed many places, with the elimination of the railroad service in the town, the closing of the factory that converted sugar beets into refined sugar, and the ferrying and wagon wheel repair, made superfluous by the modern gasoline engine.

I asked people in Perwez if they knew the Henrards' house, and they directed me to Louis Henrard's pharmacy, where I made further inquiries and learned that he lived next door. With Joan by my side, I knocked on the door and he answered.

"Can I help you?"

"Do you remember me?" I said in French.

He stared at me for a few moments. "Simon, Simon, you have

come back after all these years!"

He invited us in and we talked for a while. He told me I was the first of the eleven hidden children to return to Perwez. He called his parents' neighbors and told them I would be coming over with my wife.

The Henrards' house, which had a grocery story on the street level, was as I remembered it. I remembered the house was located next door to a butcher shop and slaughterhouse during the time I was there, housed in the 150-year-old police station. The butcher shop was still next door, and when we entered the store, I was greeted like a long-lost relative by many people who came by and sat down to tell of the adventures that had happened to me in the past. Time flew by, with the conversation going on into the early morning, and Joan and I were asked to spend the night in the neighbor's home, which was above the butcher shop. A tour of the building showed its remarkable six-foot-thick walls, its holding cells in the basement, and the wine cellar from which we imbibed a number of good Perwez wines. It was then that recollections came out from the townspeople who arrived in a constant stream.

One ugly incident was recalled by the owner of the town bakery, an anti-Semitic incident she witnessed. One of the boys I played with daily had made a comment that totally enraged me; I must have started fighting, and I was hit on the head with a play pistol and was bleeding. I was so mad that I grabbed a long, spiked rose branch in each hand and chased the boys all over town. The baker who remembered my chase had tried to stop me and clean me up, but I was angry and refused her help.

As interested as I was to hear about this incident, I didn't recall it, and it did not impact my life in the town. My school years were ones of exploration, learning, and catching up with friends. In Belgium the teaching staff, paid by the government, were priests and nuns. They were strict at times but very understanding, and I don't remember them displaying any biases. This time was very pleasant, free of care, and I was loved by an exceptional elderly couple who went far from their daily routine to feed me, clothe me, and look after my health problems.

The one health factor that had dogged me until I was seventeen years old was eczema. During trips to the doctor, I saw the war damage in the large cities such as Namur, Gembloux, and Bruxelles, but also the evidence of ongoing energetic Belgian reparations. In the Perwez house, I had my own room and, during winter weather, a brick would be heated on the wood-fired stove and then carried up to be placed under the bed covers to warm my bed. My bath required the heating of water on the pot-bellied stove and the filling of a giant wash tub, normally used for the laundry, and also warmed by the nearby stove.

The Perwez area was agricultural, with much wheat and sugar beets growing in it. The sugar beets were harvested in the fall, and I remember constant wagon loads being transported to the factory for sugar processing. The remnants of the shredded beet pulp were combined in very large stacks with used straw from the barns and the material cleaned up from the streets after transporting the sugar beets to the factory; during the winter, theses stacks were always steaming, for they became the fertilizer for the next season.

I remembered roaming in the wheat fields, in the forests, and in the town with complete freedom—the world was mine to do anything I wanted, or so it seemed to me at the time. This impacted the rest of my life: I learned to enjoy my own company and became a loner. It was hard for me to make friends casually. To my mind, a friend is someone who will lay down his life for you.

A little more about the Henrards: as I said, they were an elderly couple, and to take in a young child I think was quite a feat on their part. There is no way I can thank them. Berta was more a mother to me than anyone in my youth; she was very nurturing, so much so that the people in the town when I went back remembered her very well, how she would call for me through the streets to find out where I was and make sure that I was taken care of. She was a remarkable woman, a very strong woman for that time, if I may say so. And she ran the shop, she was the master.

These conversations and memories related to the times after the liberation on September 9, 1945, until 1948 when the Jewish organizations collected all orphans who had been hidden and had escaped deportation, and those who had no surviving parents or any relatives to collect them.

3. LIBERATION

Liberation was announced visually when the German army withdrew along the main street of the village. The retreat was hurried and not very well organized. The main logistical support must have been furnished by horses and wagons, because even at such a late date, only two German divisions were fully mechanized. The route out of town was sloped, and a wagon caught fire right in front of us because of a combination of spilled gasoline and the sparks from the horseshoes.

The following day, September 9, 1944, the first American tanks and soldiers entered the village to a very loud welcome. I remember liberation very well: the Germans were leaving helter-skelter. I was six years old at the time. To me it meant being able to go out of the house and play with the other children, widen my horizons; the exploration area was much greater, we flew our kites, and went to the school run by Catholic nuns, who were very tough again.

In December 1944, we were taken back into hiding, and it was only later that I understood what it meant: we were right in the way of the Battle of the Bulge—the largest battle in history, as it is known. Perwez was directly in the path of the German winter offensive to capture the main logistical port of the allies, namely the Port of Antwerp. It was close to the town of Bastogne, and the townspeople feared the return of the German army. It was a cold winter, so being indoors was not that bad; we had to wear ice shoes when we walked anywhere.

US Army liberation of Perwez on September 9, 1944

Citizens of Perwez posing with members of the US Army

After the allies had won the Battle of the Bulge and forced the German army to retreat back to its borders, the town celebrated its freedom by having a great a festival with rides, a shooting gallery, dance halls slides, and parades. I am guessing this was around late summer of 1945 or 1946.

This was also the time I started school which was taught by religious nuns and priests, but the content was secular, with no religious teaching that I remember. Every Friday, the nuns would give us the sweet remnants from the communion wafers.

One incident related to the liberation festival resulted in my punishment at school. I had gathered expended shells from the shooting gallery and had them in my pocket while in school. Feeling bored, I took a shell from my pocket and with a nail rubbed the inside of the shell, with my hands below the surface of the desk. Suddenly a bright blue flash and a loud bang made my classmates and the teacher jump up trying to figure out what had happened. It only took a few seconds to sort out the guilty party and I was invited to the front of the class. My punishment, which was not pleasant, was to kneel on a broomstick while holding a book in each of my outstretched arms.

In general, my life in Perwez after the liberation was one of total freedom and few cares. I cannot place specific, accurate dates to events I relate, but I had the freedom to roam the countryside and to throw myself atop the thick fields of wheat, to step on giant sugar beets that were turned into syrup; these things I could surely not have done until my seventh birthday.

While roaming around the town, I was fascinated to learn the skills and effort needed to repair wagon wheels and bombed-out buildings. In Perwez, I also learned that negatives are as much a part of life as positives.

After the war, the Henrards offered a room to an engineer who worked at the sugar beet factory. He became a person I looked up to, and one who showed me the many elements that make up the world.

I became attached to him, but after a short time, he got married and moved to a house on the street I would take to and from school. He and his wife offered to help me with my schoolwork anytime I needed it. At the time, I was no more than eight or nine years old but had already missed much education while in hiding. Their generosity was unlimited, as was the time they gave me. Shortly afterward, they welcomed a child who did not survive for long. I do not know the reasons, but I felt their heart-wrenching pain as my own, as if I had lost a sibling. Later, I witnessed the happiness of their growing family, and I saw them as a model of what family should be. When I returned decades afterward, I was happy to learn that they had had more children and had moved to Liege.

Of great ecological interest was the growing and processing of sugar beets. At the time, all the beets were hauled to the factory with the help of horses and bulls, so that at the conclusion of the harvest, the streets were deeply covered with the animal waste. After the sugar beets were processed, the remnant was just the pulp, which was returned to the farmer. Even today in the Belgian farm country in winter, you will see large stacks of heavily smoking straw that in the spring is spread all over the fields, made up of the pulp from the processed beets and any other farm organisms that have become organic fertilizer for the following year's plantings.

I was well cared for by the Henrards during my stay in Perwez, and felt wanted, even during my yearly bout with eczema. When the surviving parents came to retrieve their children, I don't recall feeling envious. According to official Belgian records, I was in Perwez until 1946.

The exact nature and time of my next residence or even how I came to the place, I do not remember. The building was located in a beautiful tree-lined boulevard with the address of 159 Avenue Winston Churchill. As it was formerly a private residence, it did not house many children in large rooms like the other orphanages I lived at. A large yard and garden surrounded the building, which permitted us to run around as we wished. The size of the bedrooms was such that we were divided into small groups. One issue I had was that I received care packages from the Henrards that I was incapable of sharing—I probably lacked trust in other people. I hoarded my care packages—I would let the food spoil rather than sharing it—and that did not help my personal relationships. It affected my ability to make friends. To this day, I'm very limited in my relationships with people.

Even though I was only at that orphanage for a short stay, I remember a number of activities from my time there: I was going to school by two trollies and changed trolleys on the Rue du Congress that had a large memorial column to Leopold I, and a newspaper shack where a weekly edition of *Tintin* came out every Thursday. On the way home, the trolley passed the royal palace. This orphanage was not orthodox, but we attended Yom Kippur services in a magnificent synagogue.

As surviving parents found their children, the orphanages were consolidated and I found myself in the Tackomoni orthodox orphanage in Antwerp, directed by a Mr. Tiefenbrunner. I estimate this was around early 1948, based on my memory of pictures from the *Jerusalem Post* on the progress of the Israeli War of Independence that were posted for all to see. I was at the Tackomoni orphanage until May 1950.

The school was next door to the orphanage, so during the day we had regular classes, then an early dinner after soccer, then two or three hours of Hebrew school. I used to stay up sometimes until midnight to do my homework, and the teachers reminded me of those nuns, they were very strict. The prayer services were deep and intense.

Tackomoni Orphanage group portrait; I am standing at far left

It was rough for a while. It was a new educational process for me, having to learn how to read Hebrew and all about the holidays. I had to learn a whole new way of life, from not being religious to being religious. I had to wear a *kippah*, and it was a strange environment. But the first time they opened a Hebrew book and showed me the writing, it looked familiar. That always stayed with me.

Over time, I began to wear a beret full-time as a head covering and became a *frum* (religious) Jew. I prayed three times a day and followed restrictive Shabbat laws. On Passover, I remember we children held the *afikoman*, the ritual piece of matzah, for ransom, as was the tradition—and were given whatever we asked for to return it so the Seder could be completed. Often we asked for trips: one year the whole orphanage went to Waterloo, and another year to the Royal Museum of Laeken.

In the summertime, we vacationed at a house on the waterfront of the Meuse River that backed onto the tree-covered mountains in the town of Dinant, a vacation lure with river access and tourist spots. The great citadel on top of the mountain overlooks the river, which serves as a highway for the transportation of goods in Europe. It was a stronghold in the defense of the country during its history and even until the world wars, for the river and road were the only way into the interior of the country.

We had access to the river by means of the ramps that gradually ran down to the water, and for me it was an opportunity to learn to swim. The slopes into the river that were used for small boat landings were perfect for splashing around and eliminated the fear of drowning. Slowly I began to move into deeper water, until I had total confidence in being able to swim.

During the school year, we walked to and from school past a synagogue that had been torched. There were burn marks on the walls and it didn't take long to ask what had happened there. We heard the names "Auschwitz and Buchenwald" in the orphanage as well, and talked about what those places meant, the parents who didn't come back. But no one asked me directly about my experiences. We were all in the same boat. There were counselors who took a liking to me and would take me away from the orphanage on the weekends for expeditions. There were also some older children there who acted as "semi-counselors." I don't think I had any expectations for my postwar life until I started going to school and there were questions about how I was going to go from A to B. The main idea in that orphanage was that if our parents did not come back, people were probably all going to Israel.

It was at this time that a very fortunate event occurred. The orphanage was sufficiently large that during the holidays, it was made available to relatives of the members of the community who wished to have a place to pray since the local synagogue had been burned. One of the people who came for services during the holidays had lived on the same street as my family before the war and must have known of me. I did not have any knowledge that my family members were still living, but he put me in touch with some relatives I had never known of, Emile Finel and his wife, Adele, who had managed to escape and had spent the war in neutral Switzerland. Emile was related to my mother and subsequently, I spent many weekends as their guest with a family life that I had never known before. Like the Henrards, they were an elderly couple who owned a butcher shop; I remember watching them make beef salami. They took me out a lot. I cannot describe their love and generosity toward me. They even purchased me a bicycle, a 28-inch model that was unique to Europe. I became very attached to that bike, as it provided me with a freedom I did not have before.

Emile and Adele Finel with me in the middle

Emile Finel was the one who notified my aunt and uncle, Mollie and Hyman Eisig, who had emigrated to the United Stated after World War I, that I had survived, and after a few months, they arranged for me to come to America. I was unhappy that I was to be sent away from everyone I knew.

I had a hernia and was not allowed to go until I had an operation, which was done between the end of March and May 16, 1950. Also, there was a lot of paperwork around trying to go. I was brought by an adult to a Belgian agency office and there was a dossier about my family: there were photographs of my parents, my brother, and my aunt; I found out how to spell my name—not *Stein* but *Steil*—and the actual date of my birthday. I had not known how old I was until then. At the time, I was very detached from this event, but since then, I've been trying to get that dossier for decades without success.

After a train trip from Antwerp, I boarded the *SS Volendam* at Rotterdam on May 16, 1950 as a "stateless person," according to the Ship's Manifest. It was a refugee ship: we were all stateless. I was still sad from leaving the orphanage and from never having said goodbye to the Henrards. I took a photo album of all the children in the orphanage, some clothes and books, and my bicycle to America.

The SS Volendam was a cruise ship completed in November 1922 and in service between Europe and the United States. The ship had a checkered career with a number of refittings to accommodate the Atlantic service. It was 575 feet long and 67.3 feet wide giving her a maximum speed of 15 knots and was built by Harland and Wolff in England. Her colorful history included barely escaping the German invasion of the Netherlands and serving the Allies in the war as a troop carrier after being in service to the Children's Overseas Reception Board. Also known as the *Kindertransport*, this group evacuated Jewish children from Germany with their parents' consent but without their presence, to save them from the Nazi laws assailing them before the war.

It is remarkable that this was the ship that brought me to the United States; it had been torpedoed and almost sank but was repaired and floated back into service by 1941. The ship was converted for troop transport in many of the Allied invasions, and carried Italian and

German prisoners as well. After the war, the ship served as transport for overseas colonial troops until 1948 when the previous route was reestablished.

The ship was far from luxurious and there was little privacy. The sleeping accommodations were still set up from the troop carrier days, meaning multi-tiered bunk beds; the food did not make any singular impressions, though the ship had a small store where snacks could be purchased, as well as grooming products and the bestselling item, watches. The voyage was monotonous: I remember no significant incidents until my arrival in New York Harbor.

4. FIRST YEARS IN AMERICA

Leaving Rotterdam on May 16, 1950, the ship traveled at maximum speed, and arrived at the site of the Statue of Liberty on May 27, 1950, with a one-day stop in Halifax, Nova Scotia, Canada. The ship docked at pier 42 of New York Harbor; Ellis Island had been closed many decades earlier. I arrived on a sunny day, and after clearing customs, I got off the ship and retrieved my luggage, including the 28-inch bicycle the Finels had given me.

My uncle, Hyman Eisig, was waiting for me, and he loaded my things into his Chrysler sedan, which impressed me. The ride home was fascinating: I watched the traffic and the sights of the ride along the ocean to Coney Island, located in the borough of Brooklyn in New York City. The "golden *medinah*" was not meaningful to me, I had no expectations. My first thought coming up the docks into the city was that Manhattan was very impressive, but the piers looked shabby; the city of Brooklyn was a bit shabby, too. But Coney Island was very neighborly. Every house had a store.

And so my life in the new world started. My Aunt Mollie and Uncle Hyman owned a row house at 3015 Mermaid Avenue and lived on the second floor. The apartment consisted of a small kitchen, master bedroom, and a dining room that connected to the living room that faced the street. There was a small yard and a store room that had once been a summer house. My bedroom was separate from the main apartment and accessed directly from the landing of the stairs leading to the rented second floor of the house. This was where I passed the next nine years or so.

On the street level were the barber shop and beauty parlor my aunt and uncle owned and managed. I was basically on my own; I did a lot of work in their shop, remodeled and painted the place. I cooked for myself. The businesses during the 1950s were different from today in that the people spent much more time in the beauty parlor and barber shops. For the women the hairstyles were time-consuming, and for the men other services such as manicuring and shaving were available. I mention this as it explains why I was so much on my own during the day: their shop hours were long and went until late into night. It was a middle-class neighborhood, people worked very hard and nothing came easily.

Though it was late in the school year, I was enrolled in the local Mark Twain Junior High School where I found I could communicate with many of the students and teachers in Yiddish. The Coney Island neighborhood consisted of two large groups of people of Jewish and Italian backgrounds, and Yiddish was the universal language of all Jewish communities in Europe and the first migrants to the U.S. after the war.

I spent my first summer exploring the neighborhoods. I passed a lot of time under the boardwalk; the beach was very nice. At the time of my arrival, Coney Island still had many remnants of the giant Luna Park amusement park that had been built early in the century. The island was also the terminal for a number of subway transit lines that allowed New Yorkers to spent much time there, and to take advantage of the beaches and the boardwalk on hot summer days. The place had rides, games, a number of salt water pools, sport facilities, and even Turkish baths.

Making friends was the biggest problem I had. Comic books became my literature and that's how I learned the English language. But I was mostly on my own.

My aunt and uncle had a married daughter, Felicia, and a son, Henry, who was a lawyer employed in upstate New York as a civil servant, running a juvenile facility. In the family picture taken in Lvov in the early 1920s, both of them are pictured.

Henry stayed on the job all week, and returned home on Fridays for the weekend, which impacted me in many ways. He required total silence and no disturbances for his reading and insisted that I could not even have the TV on. I had to make myself scarce until he left late in the evening for his club. It was as if I was not there.

Felicia was married to Sam Korn and had two children: a daughter, Anna, and a son, Danny, who was two years younger than me. This closeness in age led to problems between Danny's mother and my aunt. Felicia always took note of my technical and manual capabilities, the general shop repairs that I did over the years in my aunt and uncle's stores, and my educational interests. When the time came for me to select a college and a career, Felicia questioned my aunt: "Why let Simon go to college? He should go to work."

On the other hand, I thought my relationship with Danny over the years was friendly, and I was supportive when he decided to go to college. I believe his feelings for me were reciprocated, but they were obviously complicated by envy.

As the summer was ending, my aunt and uncle realized that—after two or more years in an orthodox orphanage in Belgium—I should have a bar mitzvah. The Jewishness of Coney Island was apparent in the monthly fundraising events of the United Jewish Appeal, the Jewish collection boxes (*pushkehs*) on the streets and in every household that were emptied monthly by religious-looking people, and the numerous synagogues. These were not grand except for one, located at the corner of 23rd and Mermaid Streets. My uncle was a member of a different synagogue on 31st Street, which he attended only on the high holidays. At the time, my religious beliefs conflicted with the family's in observance and dress. I was wearing a beret all day (as a skullcap) and had clothes which were not of the American style, that is, knickers for pants.

Consequently, my aunt and uncle decided that I would attend a neighborhood yeshiva in order to study for my bar mitzvah. The school, located at the corner of Neptune Avenue and Ocean Parkway, also taught secular subjects at the seventh-grade level. The material was not difficult for I was fluent in Hebrew text, but learning the melodies of the tropes was more challenging; I was to have a complete service including reading of the Torah and the singing of the Haftarah. The preparation for my becoming a fully-counted minyan member lasted through the winter months and until May 1951, the time of my bar mitzvah. To this day, I still remember parts of the service and its melodies, which come to me at every bar or bat mitzvah I attend. My ceremony, as is the norm, followed a Sabbath service, well attended by the congregation and many of my yeshiva friends who threw the much-anticipated candies at my head. The reception was held in my uncle's Men's Club across the street from our house, in a much less informal way than today. It was pleasant; it was more than sufficient for me.

From then on, and for the next nine years, my life was largely repetitive, with one-time events occurring only haphazardly. For the next two years, I enjoyed the neighborhood junior high school very much, with its unusual offerings of wood shop and industrial courses like printing and sheet-metal work. As I became familiar with the large and widespread New York transportation system and the reasonable costs allowing me to travel to the other boroughs, I took advantage of the many sights, museums, parks, aquariums, and avenues of the city.

My life with my aunt and uncle was limited by their time in their businesses; on work days I would eat supper with them, but my other meals were few in number until school allowed us to purchase lunch at the area candy store, a kind of sub shop as we would think of it today. For weekends, my aunt had a cook come on Friday to prepare

Sabbath and weekend meals. This was not unique in the area: it went on throughout the neighborhood. Starting Friday morning, certain vendors' activities began and were carried on until sundown. The iceman would pull up and start shaving big blocks of ice for the fish mongers, delicatessens, and butchers. The fish barrel trucks would deliver live fish. Knife sharpeners would bellow out their services as would the green grocers. All these elements of preparing for the Sabbath were very like the view of a Friday in a *shtetl* in the old country.

I went to Abraham Lincoln High School; it was a giant school, five stories high, if I remember. I played soccer, and took a full academic load, graduated with an academic diploma which indicated my hope of pursuing a college degree. Seventy percent of the school was Italian and Jewish; there were gangs with tight chinos and cigarettes rolled up in their sleeves, but they kept to themselves and we kept to ourselves and there was no trouble with being Jewish. It was very much a mixed neighborhood. The environment I lived in was very pleasant.

In New York, working papers were issued at the age of fifteen to allow young people to work in the amusement parks and restaurants in the area. Coney Island during these years attracted well-known entertainers, famous Broadway performers; in the summer, vacationing tourists arrived daily for the beaches, pools, and entertainment—and much temporary help was needed. This is how I got my first job—at Nathan's of Coney Island—which I kept for many years until my graduation from college. My first weekly paycheck, for forty-eight hours of work, was $28.35 after taxes.

I rode my bicycle everywhere in Brooklyn, until I came upon it one day with the front wheel bent, and I was not able to ride it any more. I had no idea what had happened. It was not until decades later, at a family event, that Danny confessed to me that he had been the one responsible for damaging my bike.

Aside from such small setbacks, all was stable for almost nine years, until conversations at the dinner table turned to my aunt and uncle's desire to retire and move to Florida. At the time, I still had over a year to finish my degree before graduating from college in June of 1960. It did not stop them from their plans to retire; they had only to solve where I would be living in the meantime. They had me move in with some friends, but on at least two occasions these arrangements did not last for long: one got remarried, and another couple moved in with their children. These changes made it very difficult for me to focus on my classwork, and I also lost many irreplaceable items in moving from place to place.

    I don't know who came up with the last housing recommendation, which ultimately was the best: I moved into the Young Men's Hebrew Association (YMHA) located on 92nd Street in Manhattan, where men were housed on four floors and women on three floors of the building. I was given a single room which had a single bed, a desk, and storage drawers.

5. THE YMHA

It was at the YMHA that I first realized there was much more to living and meeting people than my previous experience had indicated. The building, located at the corner of Lexington Avenue and 92nd Street in Manhattan, was more than just a place to put your head down for the night.

The residents of the Y consisted of young people who were in the middle of their college education, or at special programs such as the Fashion Institute of New York, or had just graduated and were pursuing advanced degrees in their specialties. One of the outcomes of the three-year limit for living at the Y was that a large community of former residents moved from there out into the immediate neighborhood and as far as Greenwich Village. These were people with a wide range of knowledge, capabilities, and interests that gave rise to many interesting conversations.

The halls of the building were at times filled with the sounds of popular and "long-hair" music, and many discussions were held in the larger bedrooms on the topic of the day, in English and in many foreign languages. I met people who came from various regions of the United States with different backgrounds and beliefs, and at times with physical disabilities. I remember a young man named Arthur who had been afflicted with polio; he had graduated with a teaching degree and wanted to teach in New York City, but since his disability prevented him from raising his arm, the City could not employ him. He was so committed that he found a job in the school system of a neighboring county. What a person.

At the Y, I involved myself in the simple joys of life, swimming and sunbathing, learning how to dance, and taking in the entertainment, plays and movies, and the magnificent museums and sites.

I met a fellow engineer, Robert Spear, whose mother had passed on and his relationship with his stepmother was not satisfactory. The similarities in our backgrounds—having to deal with maternal figures other than our own mothers—led us to become friends. We spent much time in joint activities, eating out and taking in shows on Sunday afternoons.

The Y had also had many other activities of which I partook as a resident. The Kaufman auditorium was well known for attracting many show business and opera performers, such as Richard Tucker, the famous cantor, for example—and there were often free tickets for residents. The exercise room, the roof deck area, and the arts and craft area were also available to any resident.

Even with all these perks, I had certain monetary responsibilities, such as rent, food, and later, car insurance and maintenance. Prior to my graduation, I continued to work at Nathan's Famous hot dog concession stand in Coney Island. When I started working there at the age of fourteen, I worked full-time during the summer months; later, I worked part-time in the winter months as well. My duties were simple at the beginning, but evolved into responsibility for food preparation, both in the kitchen and on the customer service counter. The salary was more than satisfactory, but while I was still in school and living at the Y, I was able to earn no more than $20 for a weekend of work. The availability of work depended on good weather that attracted people to the businesses and amusements on the boardwalk and beach.

Three young ladies, two of them graduates from Brandeis University, came to the YMHA. One returned to Boston, and the other two, both brilliant mathematicians, stayed on. One of them later headed the AT&T computer laboratory and I came across her during my career travels. Sadly, she lost her battle with cancer. The other, named Susan, married my friend Robert Spear; I went on many double dates with them and the woman who ultimately became my wife, Joan Davida Smigel.

How I met my future wife is a short story in itself. After a June graduation from the Polytechnic Institute of Brooklyn with a degree in Mechanical Engineering, I finally began earning a livable salary as a civil servant with the United States Navy Laboratory, and I felt wealthy enough to go on a vacation. In those years, the Catskill Mountains in upstate New York were dotted with a variety of vacation hotels that served the many layers of society. The Laurels Country Club was a hotel for young, upwardly mobile men and women, with swimming, tennis, and other sports activities, and entertainers who rotated through the region. In the evenings after dinner, all the guests would gather and meet casually, evaluating members of the opposite sex who might pique their interests. And so I spied Joan, acting mother-like toward many other girls, at one of these soirees.

My interest in her was based on the idea that I wanted an independent woman, maybe because of my own independence throughout my life, and she accepted my invitation to that night's show. We spent a couple of days together, and at the end of the weekend we both agreed to meet again on our return home. She lived in Queens, and that meant I had to make significant use of public transportation or purchase a car, which I shortly did.

6. DATING AND MARRIAGE

Upon my return to New York City from the Catskills, I debated whether to keep my word and call Joan: we had had a very pleasant time at the Laurels, swimming and playing a bit of tennis, walking and talking and attending the many entertainments in the days and evenings. All the same, I must admit I did not call her the following week, but took a couple of weeks to cogitate on whether I was ready to pursue dating seriously.

Finally, I took a deep breath and called her for a date the next Saturday. At that point, I had purchased but not yet received delivery of my car, so I had to get to her house by subway and then a bus running along Union Turnpike. Since I picked her up at her house, I immediately met her family: her father, David Smigel, her mother, Miriam, and her sister, Judith. They lived in a two-family abode with Joan's uncle and his children on the first floor, and Joan's family on the second floor.

I was very proud to have such a beautiful girl on my arm. Our early dates consisted of going to neighborhood attractions such as taking in a movie, followed with eating out in a local cozy Italian restaurant; when the date went on into the early morning hours, we stopped and purchased fresh bagels and the Sunday edition of *The New York Times*. Occasionally, I slept over and spent the next day at Joan's house, ending in a tiring trip back to the Y.

Time passed quickly. During these months, Joan and I double-dated numerous times with Robert and Susan, usually taking in a Broadway show followed by a walk to a restaurant in the city. But that first significant amount of money in my pocket from my engineering job must have started me dreaming about seeing the world, and feeling that I was not ready for marriage. Around the early part of 1961, I broke off seeing Joan.

My new job involved developing state-of-the-art inertial navigation systems in a newly-established classified laboratory that was part of the Brooklyn Naval Shipyard guarded by a Marine Corps security section. The effort of doing this work was more on my mind than social relations; dating with the goal of marriage was of limited interest to me in the first months of the job.

As the summer arrived, many of the young students living at the Y returned to their homes, taking the energy of the place with them. Without its concerts, lectures, and residents, it became a very boring place, with few options for casual dating. I went on a number of less-than-satisfactory dates, and the thought of my past happy times with Joan made me want to find out what she was doing. As September rolled in, I decided to give her a call.

What can I say except that we just clicked? I found Joan to be an independent soulmate, and I wanted to spend my future with her. We were engaged on March 31, 1962. Our wedding was held in the recently-renovated Aperion Manor on Kings Highway in Brooklyn, NY. The place has a beautiful marble staircase like a movie set, and her appearance gliding down those stairs was movie-like, too. The Jewish ceremony under the *chuppah*, and the signing of the *ketubah* (traditional marriage contract) made me think about my family that was not there. Though my aunt and uncle walked me down the aisle, and more aunts and uncles, cousins, and friends were present, my thoughts, I must admit, were elsewhere. Why had I survived?

Still, the reception was well planned and we all had a very enjoyable time. Joan and I planned to leave for our honeymoon at the end of the reception, and here we set the precedent for all our future travels: we just hit the road without any reservations, but with the general idea of going to Canada by way of New York and returning through New England.

On our wedding day, August 12, 1962

7. WORK AND FAMILY

Joan and I were married on August 12, 1962 and departed for our honeymoon the next day, having spent the night at our already-rented garden apartment at a development called the Cloverdale Gardens. Our second-floor apartment had two bedrooms, a large living room, a small kitchen, a bath, and a small porch. Not grand, but cozy.

Our trip consisted of driving upstate through New York towards Albany, veering to Montreal and on to Quebec. From Quebec returning to the United States at Rouses Point customs, continuing on to New England and Massachusetts, Rhode Island, Connecticut and finally Queens, New York to our apartment. The first day we did not get very far, for we stopped for the night after driving to the end of the Hariman Thruway, at Lake George, Fort William and Mary to satisfy my historical interests. Our next stop was at a very smoky motel, due to a brush fire, in Plattsburg, NY, at the time a noisy Strategic Air Command Airforce base. We planned to go next to Montreal, the site of a World Exposition that we had not attended but were curious to compare to the Flushing, New York site of the 1938 Exposition. When we crossed into Canada, I was cross-examined by the Customs officials due to my accent, but allowed to enter the country. Since our goal was Quebec, we pushed on and stopped at the Cardinal Motel just outside of the city. The motel was convenient, and in later years we always looked for it and stayed there on trips with our friends.

After strolling in Quebec's old city we decided to take a tour of the castle which at the time was also a training station for new military cadets. A squad of cadets were marching by, and the stream of whistles at Joan just made me proud of having such a beautiful wife on my arm. The next day we ambled through the lower city, which had been repaired and made to recreate the city around the time of the British capture.

Heading back to the US, Joan and I avoided a serious car accident because of a premonition I had upon arriving at a crossroad. I decided to stop there, and just at that moment a car sped by in front of us; it failed to make the turn and jetted into the gas station across the street, then crossed a ditch and slammed into stacks of car tires that stopped it. I confirmed that the occupants were not hurt and offered a ride, but they indicated that arrangements for their pickup had been made. The story did not end here: I did not let the townspeople know that I had knowledge of French—but it was clear they felt that I was responsible for the accident. When the police arrived, I spoke in French and explained what had happened, and only then did I feel that their notion of this possibility began to subside, and the police ended by saying that I had had no responsibility for the accident.

We crossed into the US at Rouse's Point on the way to Vermont, where we had an overnight stay at a beautiful motel and restaurant. The motel was a set of buildings with the main rooms in a converted barn. The inside was covered with polished wood, and the second floor was still sloped from the original hay loft. Our room included an old spring mattress at the level of a window; when I first jumped onto the bed, I almost flew out of the window. The home-cooked breakfast with the local maple syrup was delicious and made for memories.

And so we carried on with our drive through the New England states with all of their historical places. Our target for a longer stop was the state of Rhode Island. During our wedding, a cousin of Joan's who lived in Newport, Rhode Island had invited us to visit and stay for the ongoing America's Cup sailing races. Newport at the time was going through an economic downturn because the US Navy had closed its facility in the area, resulting in real estate difficulties and a glut of antiques. Joan and I spent some time looking for bargains and came up with a beautiful brass microscope and an Edison-type cylinder record player. When I closed our house after Joan died, I passed the microscope to my son, Evan, the doctor in the family.

We saw that there were good opportunities for real estate purchases in Newport, but neither of us had jobs there. We spent a number of days watching the America's Cup races with all of their excitement, and feasting on the local seafood with fish, shrimp, and not to leave out New England lobsters. The weather in August was beautiful and we were regretful at having to leave Newport. The slow ride home took us onto the Connecticut Parkway, across the Verrazano Bridge to our apartment in Queens, NY and a well-earned rest.

We resumed our lives: Joan had a position as a laboratory nurse in the hospital and I continued as an engineer at the Brooklyn Navy Yard. Since I had lived in Manhattan and enjoyed the entertainment it offered, Joan and I tried to partake in the same pastimes, but soon realized that commuting into the city during the week was not to be undertaken too often. The time it took to go back and forth from work to home and then to the city and home just resulted in too little sleep at night.

The year ended with Joan announcing that we were going to be parents. The following months were spent in the usual purchase of baby items from furniture to clothing. The prospective grandparents, Miriam and Dave Smigel, were excited and worried. The happy event occurred on July 25, 1963 when Adam Martin Steil was born.

At this time I had been with the civil service more than three years, which gave me the opportunity to return to any such job in the future. I was beginning to be interested in broadening my work experience by obtaining a position with an industrial company.

After searching and being offered positions in Florida and Minnesota, I chose Florida—I guess for the weather—since I had already been to Minnesota in the winter. On the road to Florida, Adam celebrated his first birthday at the Carolina Restaurant.

For about a year, we lived in a low-rent home with no air conditioning which made it possible for us to take advantage of the tourist sites, such as an alligator farm, Silver Springs, Tarpon Springs, and many waterfront sights. I worked at Martin Marietta on sensitive and challenging programs while Joan was a stay-at-home mother. Shortly after we moved there, Joan announced we were expecting again. Evan Neil Steil was born on February 9, 1965 in Florida Hospital Orlando. I cannot say whether his sunny disposition had anything to do with the weather as he was growing up.

All seemed to be going along well until I began having breathing problems. These did not resolve until after our departure from Florida, nor did we know the reasons for the problem at the time. But since it seemed to be environmental, I applied for a position with the Northrop company in Norwood, Massachusetts. During our stay in that state we purchased our first house, and our other two sons were born, Alexander Paul on December 21, 1967 and Douglas Harlan on January 10, 1970, both at Framingham Hospital.

Our time in Massachusetts was one of extreme happiness in raising our children; the townspeople were genuinely friendly, and there was the unique feature in that state that gave authority to each person to vote for the taxes and rules of their town. In winter, we skated in our backyard, and in the warmer weather we took advantage of the historical sites to further educate ourselves and to appreciate this country.

When I went to work at MIT, my older children could take advantage of the MIT summer camp nearby, which involved driving them to work with me. The camp taught my children how to sail on the Charles River, introduced them to scientific wonders, and gave my wife some peaceful moments. An opportunity for an advance in responsibility resulted in my working for the Raytheon Company followed by assignments with other industrial non-military companies.

The end of the space program resulted in a draw-down of work along the 128 technical corridor and my need to look for a new position. Unfortunately, the only position I could get was to go back to the US Navy job in New York, requiring that I commute for a short while and ultimately that we sell our first house. Shortly after I started work, an announcement was made that the personnel and job were to be transferred to the US Naval Development Center in Pennsylvania.

As Joan and I were beginning to look at purchasing a house in Nassau county, New York, we had to find a way to verify the rumor that I would be transferred again soon, since purchasing and selling the same house within a year would be an expensive proposition. Joan's cousin in Newport, Rhode Island, came up as a source of information on whether the rumor could be confirmed, based on the fact that she had been friends for many years with the naval personnel attached to the base. She gave us an open answer not to purchase a house in the near future; shortly afterward, we received the official word.

Our one-year stay in the small Floral Garden apartment was not one that I had looked forward to, since we also had to use it for the storage of our furniture and goods. The announcement allowed us to search for a future home in Bucks County, Pennsylvania. We found a newly constructed house at 25 Netherlands Drive, Holland, PA, and were promised a short delivery date.

Our move—also reimbursed by the government—was as smooth as we could expect, and we undertook it happily. Normal home life allowed the children free movement in the surrounding land, and their school environment was made familiar by the number of fellow New York laboratory workers who had also purchased homes in the area.

The time passed quickly, and we took in the history of the state with visits to reenactments of Washington Crossing the Delaware, the last campground of the Continental Army in New Jersey, Atlantic City beaches and boardwalks, antiquing in Upper New Hope, and taking advantage of the Princeton actors showing Gilbert and Sullivan staged shows in the park across the Delaware river.

For the first ten years, Joan continued as a homemaker. But she had observed much about nursing when she worked at a hospital before our marriage, and while we were in Pennsylvania, she decided she wanted to become a registered nurse. She enrolled at Bucks County Community College and graduated in the early seventies.

During a foul-weather day, our son Evan entered a contest in a local newspaper requiring him to write a short essay on a family wish. Surprisingly, he was declared a winner with another neighbor's son, coincidentally also named Steil—Evan and Kevin were joint winners—and both families enjoyed a fully paid day at Great Adventure Amusement Park in New Jersey.

When I shared my story with them (as best I knew it in 1976), the fact that our families had identical names brought up the question of whether we were related. Even though we were of different religious persuasions, it was an open question. The other Steils had mentioned some past discussions by their grandmother about religious issues such as conversions, but by the time of our meeting she had died, so nothing could be confirmed. Still, there were interesting genetic similarities, namely we were both missing eye teeth and shared some identical physical features: David Steil (Kevin's father) and I looked quite alike. After that, our families met a number of times, and we received an invitation to visit the rest of the family in St Cloud, Minnesota. We gladly accepted.

One outstanding event in 1976 was the bar mitzvah of our eldest, Adam, who made us and the family very proud. I always felt the responsibility of passing on my faith to my family because of the history of the war and the destruction of the Steil and Finel family members in Lvov. Evan had his bar mitzvah in 1978 in Pennsylvania as well. Alexander and Douglas had their bar mitzvahs in 1980 and 1983 respectively in Burke, Virginia.

The family spent a total of five happy years in Buck's County until once again the same rumors of government closings began to circulate. We left Buck's County in the fall of 1978 and our children's ages were: Adam—fifteen, Evan—thirteen, Alexander—ten, and Douglas—eight years old. I must admit that I had become dissatisfied with my position at NADC for lack of any advancement. I was offered a temporary position in Washington with the Navy office responsible for basic research and development; I had to demonstrate and select technologies that would further the capabilities of the US Navy and manage those programs that were selected. The position required me to commute from Philadelphia to Washington on a weekly basis and stay in a hotel for four nights a week.

But things continued to fall into place for me. A new joint Cruise Missiles program management office was being established and since rumors of the closing of NADC were circulating, I again ventured to look for a permanent position in Washington. After the usual selection process I was offered one of two positions, one of them a supervisory role at a higher grade, which I opted for. The search for a new home with the other new employees resulted in many of us finding homes in a newly-developed area called Burke Center in Fairfax, Virginia. So we moved to a motel: a cat, a dog, four children and two adults. It was a bit cramped for space but we survived knowing that the government was paying for our motel for thirty days—and then thirty more—while our house in the rural development was being finished.

The new program had such a high priority that the work was exciting, with many new responsibilities and challenges. Unfortunately, it all came to an end after the dissolution of the joint office and the shifting of the authority to individual services. As luck would again be on my side, I received a promotion and went to work for the Material Command of the Army as a weapons system staff manager with singular communications abilities with the military high command. As an example, I was on a committee of NATO members required to travel to Brussels twice a year to represent the United States. In the following year I attended the Defense Systems Management College where I honed my management skills. Eventually, I retired from the civil service and worked in a number of jobs with private contractors but always supporting the defense department.

During this time, Joan graduated as a nurse and started her new career at the George Washington Medical Center in the District of Columbia, and we took turns taking care of the family. Looking back at the uncertain or difficult times I had in my relationships with my beloved Joan and my children, one issue that was raised repeatedly and is still raised even years after Joan's passing, was how we made decisions to resolve our children's questions and conflicts. This is probably the most difficult part of this biography that I decided to write. The trouble that any parents have in raising their children is that the answers put forth are not of one voice. It is well known that it does not take long for the children to recognize where the answer they are looking for can be gotten, that is, which parent, either father or mother, would be the one to resolve these issues. When decisions had to be made in our family, I have been characterized as deferring to my wife.

The easiest excuse for me is blaming all parenting failures on having been orphaned at a very early age, and never having had the benefit of parental experience to guide me during my formative years. I am not looking for an excuse nor a reason to blame anybody. But being an orphan certainly affected my personal attitudes, and my living conditions as a child firmed up these attitudes.

When the time came for me to consider marriage, I asked myself the question of what type of wife I should be looking for. The answer was not one that came to me immediately, but it became apparent when I was actively dating after graduation, and as my financial independence emerged.

The conditions during the war required me to be on my own, and not to have anyone close to me to ask for help, or to make decisions for me. The nine years I lived with my uncle and aunt were also years that did not expose me to family decision-making dynamics. Their two children were already on their own. My relationship with Felicia encompassed very few invitations to her house and few invitations to joint events with her son, even though Danny and I were close. As for Henry's relationship with me after arriving home, there was none: he would spend the time at his professional club in Coney Island. In other words, I would see him and say hello, and at the end of the weekend when he was going back to his job, I would say goodbye.

So, my experience in the resolution of outstanding issues in marriage such as the raising of children in a two-parent environment was nonexistent. As my marriage progressed, it became clear to me that Joan's independence in addressing issues without my input was a problem. I did not expect that decisions were to be made mutually at all times, but I felt that those that involved the children did have to be mutual, and so when the children asked me for something, I always told them to ask their mother, hoping that she would discuss it with me for an answer we could both agree upon. The children took advantage of knowing that I would tell them to ask Joan, and my hopes of a mutual resolution were not apparent, nor were my considerations of the impact my decisions would have on the marriage. Instead, the children saw me as deferring to Joan at all times. I must admit now that this was a mistake; there were issues I should have pursued even with the risk of a negative outcome.

When I became a parent, I also realized that no one had been there in my own childhood to teach me about the problems and solutions of growing up, and I wanted my children to accumulate such knowledge without having to go through the experiences of those problems themselves. But the result of my trying to provide such insights was that my talks were often seen as "lecturing." I had hoped that they would start their lives from a higher level of knowledge and wisdom than I did, and perhaps I failed to understand that each child must learn by his own experience the directions he will take in his lifetime.

Soon enough, the elder children were graduating high school and were interested in attending college. As Joan was an employee of George Washington University, one great benefit was that our children could attend the university at no cost.

Commuting from Virginia was a problem, though, and we realized it made sense to purchase a brownstone in the District and renovate it for our sons, who would share the rental costs with other students. At the time, such a purchase was still financially feasible. As we searched for a house and waited to find out whether Adam had been admitted to GWU, an unexpected event happened to me. While I was at work with a government contractor, I began to have sharp chest pains, sweating, and serious heartburn. When the pains hung on, I called Joan who immediately drove over to bring me to the emergency center of Alexandria Hospital. The doctors told us that I had had a heart attack. Further tests indicated that I had been very lucky, since there was no lasting damage. After a week I was dismissed from the hospital with the usual medications and the recommendation to be physically active. Joan began to be more careful with the food she prepared for me, and I watched my food intake. I increased my activity level by working on house renovations.

With no long-term consequences of my heart attack, we started the renovation of the house the following week. I worked on them for at least four hours a day after work, and for twelve hours each day on the weekend. The idea worked out satisfactorily for a time, with the two older children, Adam and Evan, using the renovated house as their address, and sharing it with two or three additional students.

Ultimately, Evan graduated from the university, and Adam, our eldest, took a break before continuing his studies and completing his bachelor's and master's degrees. Evan furthered his studies with a master's degree from the University of Virginia and then obtained an

MD from the University of Pittsburgh medical school.

The younger two, Alexander and Douglas, completed their public education at Robinson High School in Fairfax, Virginia, from which Adam and Evan had also graduated.

Douglas spent three years at Northern Virginia Community College working through a number of specific interests, and finally decided to obtain a degree in geology, not from George Washington University, but from the University of Maryland which had a better program for his interests.

Alexander took a different route in his education. His interests were piqued at the start of the computer and technology revolution, which came with the requirement for constant training in the latest applications and security knowledge. He obtained certain certifications in the knowledge and applications of hardware and networking, and these gained him entry to private industry and government positions.

Adam took a little longer to find his direction in his short life. He earned his master's degree in international studies and started on his doctorate, and many special courses that were required for his work in the intelligence community supporting national security operations. Based on his honors and recommendations and the comments of his fellow workers, he was brilliant. His personal success was apparent to me each time he came home from his business trips and brought me a small gift that indicated the importance and seriousness of the national responsibilities in his hands.

In 2009, Joan and I were in a car accident on the highway; I was only bruised, but Joan was not wearing a seatbelt, and she was badly injured. After that, her health declined steadily; as a heavy smoker, she had trouble with her heart as well, and her mobility become impaired.

In 2012, we celebrated our fiftieth wedding anniversary with our children and grandchildren, and felt the pride of having made a full and rich life together.

Our fiftieth wedding anniversary celebration, August 2012

With Joan on our fiftieth anniversary, August 2012

With my sons, Douglas and Adam, at the US Holocaust Memorial Museum twentieth anniversary celebration, April 2013

In April of 2013, I was invited to attend the twentieth anniversary of the United States Holocaust Memorial Museum, whose inaugural opening twenty years earlier I had also been invited to as a special guest, along with other survivors and refugees from that time, to celebrate the triumph of our survival and to remember all those who had not come out of the Shoah alive.

Joan's health had continued to decline in the years since our accident, and after a long up-and-down battle with congestive heart failure and stays in many hospitals around Northern Virginia, she died on September 5, 2013.

Eight short days later, Adam died at the age of fifty, as the result of an apparent heart attack. We did not order an autopsy so we were not certain of the cause of his death. We were still sitting *shiva* for Joan when we got the news about Adam. Between Rosh Hashanah and Yom Kippur, we continued our *shiva* for him. We all felt disbelief and shock, and I felt the particular grief of burying my firstborn son. Adam had never married; his life was cut off much too early. He was beginning to reap the fruits of his hard work, and had recently become involved in a new relationship and begun to look forward to family life. His popularity was indicated by the large number of stones placed on his grave, a Jewish tradition that his friends and family upheld each time they visited.

But in the years before that, there were many memorable incidents, both funny and lucky, in raising a family of four boys. Not many parents would receive telephone calls from neighbors in panicked voices stating that their son was riding his bicycle with a snake wrapped around the handlebars. One of our boys almost set a neighbor's house on fire when a Fourth of July firecracker jumped into a dried pine tree at the entrance to the garage. A quick pail of water averted the tragedy.

An even more serious incident, that luckily did not result in physical injury to the children involved, occurred when they tried to use building materials as toys. The new neighborhood had straw bales at its building site on which the children decided to build a playhouse. The idea was inventive, but lighting a match in the straw house was not wise. We parents repaid the damage to the straw.

There was one incident Joan and I only learned about when some of our children tried to leave the house dressed in clothing they would not usually wear on school days. It turned out their reason for dressing up was that they were scheduled for a day in court. The story took a while to come out: the neighborhood children were playing with laser tag pistols and rifles on school grounds after dark. Assuming they were trespassers, some residents called the police. Tragedy could have resulted from the fact that the police working in the dark assumed that weapons were in the hands of the children; the saving grace was that the children instantly stopped moving when ordered to do so. This incident echoes even today with the ongoing issue of police-civilian communications.

As the boys began to drive we furnished them with cars, so that ultimately, we had six cars and a spare in the driveway. The cost of maintaining them was eased by their mechanical interest in doing the repairs themselves. In one case, this resulted in a unique modification to a sedan that once again brought police attention. One of the boys had taken a Sawzall and cut the frame from the section behind the driver's seat off the car, moved the seats into the trunk area, and reinstalled all the safety belts. The police stopped them, but there was no citation given, since it had all been done according to safety regulations.

With my sons and grandsons, November 2017

But what matters most is this: Joan and I raised our children through these many interesting, funny, and sometimes dangerous events—the overall challenges of parenting—but we were blessed with sons who grew to manhood without falling into the traps of drug use or other serious misbehaviors. They all found their way forward.

We spent many happy years together in the house in Burke Center, Fairfax County, until the now-grown children began to leave the coop permanently. Evan became engaged and married Linda Sell in 1992. Douglas married Amy Blivess in 1997 and Alexander married Saltanat Ospanov in 2006. We happily welcomed seven grandchildren into the family, and eventually celebrated the marriage of one granddaughter, Evan's daughter, Rebeccah, to Roy Levy from Israel.

Rebeccah wanted to get married in Israel, since her groom came from there, but she was certain she would be barred, as she had always assumed her mother, Linda, wasn't Jewish; yet Linda's mother, Eva, had told stories of her own mother, Irene, lighting Shabbat candles and observing some of the other Jewish traditions. It also developed that Rebeccah's grandmother had written an unpublished book about her experiences during the war, and one of the stories in the book revealed that her great-grandmother had worn a yellow star.

The Steil family in Israel, November 2017

With all my years of experience, I was able to help Rebeccah with her own genealogical research. We went way beyond the scope of Jewishgen.com, and finally, through the Reform Hungarian Church and other sources, we found her great-great-grandparents and were able to determine that they had indeed been Jewish. Still, we had no documentation specifically proving Irene's religion. So Rebeccah flew to Hungary and located archival records of the German occupation that indicated her great-grandmother had been declared Jewish by the German government, and she obtained a letter of confirmation to that effect from the chief rabbi of Hungary. This meant Rebeccah, too, was a Jew by law, and she was able to marry in Israel in November 2017, with all of us in attendance.

I wrote to her mother and said, "Welcome to the tribe."

BIBLIOGRAPHY

Brachfeld, Silvain. *Ils n'ont pas eu ces gosses: L'histoire de plus de 500 enfants juifs sans parents fichés à la Gestapo et placés pendant l'occupation allemande dans les homes de l'association des juifs de Belgique (You Didn't Get These Children: The history of the more than 500 orphaned Jewish children taken by the Gestapo and placed during the German occupation in the homes of the Jewish Association of Belgium)*. Brussels, Belgium. Institut de Récherche Sur le Judaïsme Belge, 1989.

Brachfeld, Silvain. *Merci de Nous Avoir Sauvés. Temoignages d'Enfants Juifs Caches en Belgique (Thank you for Saving Us. Testimonies of Jewish Children Hidden in Belgium)*. Brussels, Belgium. Institut De Recherche Sur Le Judaisme Belge, 2007.

Brachfeld, Silvain. *The Brachfeld Family Book, A Gift of Life: The Deportation and the Rescue of the Jews in Occupied Belgium (1940-1944)*. Antwerp, Belgium. Institute for Research on Belgian Judaism, 2007.

Klarsfeld, Serge and Steinberg, Maxime. *Memorial de la déportation des juifs de Belgique (Memorial of the Deportation of the Jews of Belgium)*. Union des déportés juifs en Belgique et filles et fils de la deportation. New York, NY. Beate Klarsfeld Foundation, 1982.

United States Holocaust Memorial Museum website:
https://www.ushmm.org.

Wikipedia entry, "SS Volendam" last edited 12/28/2018:
https://en.wikipedia.org/wiki/SS Volendam.

Yad Vashem Archive:
https://www.yadvashem.org/archive.html.

www.ingramcontent.com/pod-product-compliance
Lightning Source LLC
Chambersburg PA
CBHW040311050426
42449CB00019B/3483